This Book Belongs To

_____

This book is dedicated to Tony who loves spending time with the kids at arcades.
- P.L.

Me on the Page Publishing
Copyright © 2018 Phelicia Lang

ISBN-13: 978-1-7338064-1-1

Illustrations Copyright © Phelicia Lang

Book Design by Cassandra Bowen, Uzuri Designs
www.uzuridesigns.com

Tay

By Phelicia Lang

Book 5

AN EARLY
READER SERIES

Illustrated by
Samanta Veliz

Reading Tips

Dear Family,

You are your child's first teacher! Be sure to spend time reading to and with them each day. They also need you to listen to them read. When they are reading, if they get stuck on a word, teach them to use these simple strategies on the next page. Give them some think time before you give them the answer. Soon your little reader will be reading longer and harder books.

Enjoy your child and Happy Reading!

Phelicia Lang

If your child gets stuck on a word...

Look at the picture	👀
Touch each letter and say its sound slowly	bag
Go back and re-read	↩
Skip the word and come back to it	bag and
Go back and read it again	↩

Remember to always think...

- Does my word make sense?
- Does my word look right?
- Does my word sound right?

Tay Goes to the Go Karts

This is Tay.

He is smart.

He likes to spend time with his family.

Today is Saturday and Tay has cleaned his room. His mom and dad are proud.

Tay likes cars.

He will go on a drive

with his family.

Tay and his sister see the family ride and games.

This will be a lot of fun!

They wait safely
while waiting for
their tickets.

His dad checks to see
if Tay is tall enough
to ride.

Yay!! He can ride.

Go karts are very loud!
Tay will ask
for special ear plugs.

Go karts have four
wheels and can
go very fast!

They will all have
to wear seatbelts and
helmets. They put
them on.

They are finally
ready. Off they go!!!!

Tay goes around
and around the
racetrack safely.
He stays in his lane.

Tay's dad goes
faster and faster.

Bump!

He bumps into Tay!

Tay chases him
but his time is up.

His family has finished
their laps around
the track and must
let others ride.

It is time to go home.

Tay thanks his mom and dad for the special day.
They have a big family hug.

Tay had fun
at the go karts.

Tay loves go karts!

About the Author

Phelicia is a loving wife to Tony, mother to four wonderful children and a precious grandson. They have all inspired her journey to find good books to reflect their lives and interests.

As a Reading Specialist she's passionate about finding the right books to help readers connect to stories they love and books that reflect the readers.

Dreaming big dreams and using those dreams and gifts to help others, is the message she shares with her students.

When she's not creating on her computer she can be found Dreaming Big Dreams, reading and shopping.

CPSIA information can be obtained
at www.ICGtesting.com
Printed in the USA
LVHW072019160920
666191LV00001B/35

9 781733 806411

3 1901 06189 4780